D1034971

SAVING WILDLIFE

Rain Forest Animals

by Sonya Newland

A⁺
Smart Apple Media

Published by Smart Apple Media
P.O. Box 3263, Mankato, Minnesota 56002

Printed in the United States of America at Corporate Graphics,
in North Mankato, Minnesota.

Published by arrangement with the
Watts Publishing Group Ltd., London.

Library of Congress Cataloging-in-Publication Data
Newland, Sonya.
 Rain forest animals / by Sonya Newland.
   p. cm. -- (Saving wildlife)
 Includes bibliographical references and index.
 Summary: "Presents the harmful effects deforestation, global warming, and hunting have on endangered species of tropical and
temperate rain forest ecosystems. Introduces conservation efforts and ways for readers to get involved. Includes maps, diagrams,
and reading quiz"--Provided by publisher.
 ISBN 978-1-59920-660-8 (library binding)
 1. Rain forest animals--Juvenile literature. 2. Wildlife conservation--Juvenile literature. I. Title.
 QL112.N39 2012
 591.734--dc22

                            2010027174

Produced for Franklin Watts by
White-Thomson Publishing
Series consultant: Sally Morgan
Designer: Clare Nicholas
Picture researcher: Amy Sparks

Contents

Words in **bold** are in the glossary on page 31.

What Is a Rain Forest?

Rain forests are areas of thick forest where it rains nearly all year round. They are home to more than half of all the millions of types of plants and animals on earth.

▶ *This map shows the areas of tropical and temperate rain forests. Although they only cover a small part of the earth, they are home to more than half of all living things.*

Salamander
(page 21)

● Tropical rain forest

● Temperate rain forest

Golden lion
tamarin
(page 12)

Warm and Cool Rain Forests

There are two types of rain forest. Tropical rain forests are found close to the **equator**, where it is always warm. Plants grow quickly in the hot, damp conditions, providing food and shelter for animals as large as tigers and as small as ants. Temperate rain forests are often found along coasts and on mountain slopes. These forests are home to creatures that prefer a cooler **climate**, such as bears, deer, and otters.

Three-toed sloth
(page 15)

The goliath birdeaters of the South American rain forest are the largest spiders in the world. Some of them are bigger than a dinner plate!

← 12 in. (30 cm) →

A High-rise Home

Rain forests are divided into layers. At the bottom is the dark, damp forest floor, where creatures such as spiders, scorpions, and beetles live. Above this, there are small trees and bushes growing toward the sunlight. The tops of the trees are called the **canopy**. This layer of the rain forest is buzzing with life. Monkeys swing between the trees, butterflies flutter among the flowers, and snakes curl around the branches. Above the very tallest trees, eagles soar, looking for prey in the canopy below.

Bengal tiger (page 10)

Tropic of Cancer

Equator

Tropic of Capricorn

Javan rhino (page 9)

Forest elephant (page 8)

Rain Forests under Threat

Huge areas of the world's rain forests are being cut down. People want the land to live on, to grow crops, and to graze livestock. They also want to make use of the wood from the trees.

Homeless and Hungry

People are worried about the destruction of the rain forests because it contributes to **global warming**, but the destruction also has a huge effect on the forest animals. Without the trees, many creatures lose their homes. The flowers, fruit, and leaves of the trees also provide food for millions of animals. No trees means no food.

▼ *Cutting down the rain forests affects the environment and leaves animals without food or shelter.*

WHAT DO YOU THINK?

In Southeast Asia, parts of the rain forest are being cut down to make way for oil palm **plantations**. The oil is used to make environmentally-friendly vehicle fuels. What arguments do you think there are for and against using rain forest land in this way?

Separation and Competition

When parts of the rain forest are cleared, groups of animals can become separated from others of their **species**. This is called **fragmentation**, and it reduces the number of potential mates for the animals. As more creatures are forced to live in smaller areas of forest, there is greater competition for food, water, and shelter. There may not be enough to go around.

Human Hunters

Hunting is also a threat to rain forest animals such as tigers, caimans, and rhinos. Some people kill them for their valuable meat, fur, or horns, but others just hunt them for sport. The people who live in and around the rain forests are often respectful of their environment, but sometimes they feel they must cut down the trees or kill the animals to survive.

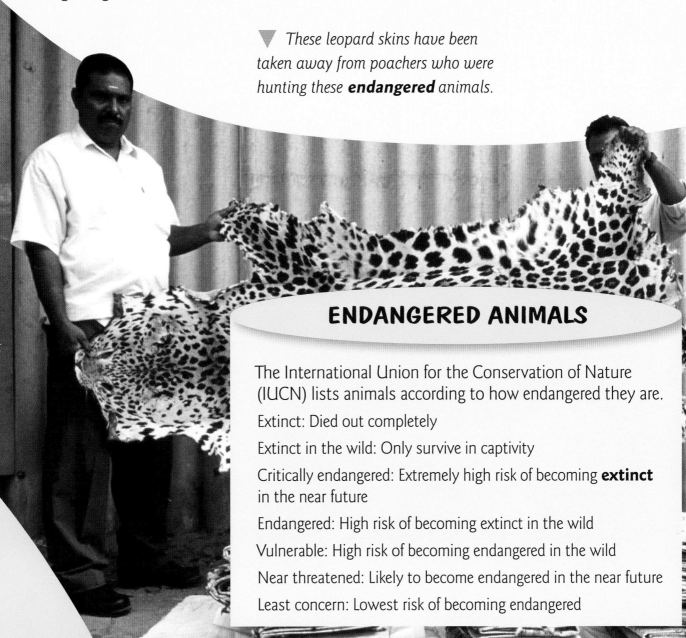

▼ *These leopard skins have been taken away from poachers who were hunting these **endangered** animals.*

ENDANGERED ANIMALS

The International Union for the Conservation of Nature (IUCN) lists animals according to how endangered they are.

Extinct: Died out completely

Extinct in the wild: Only survive in captivity

Critically endangered: Extremely high risk of becoming **extinct** in the near future

Endangered: High risk of becoming extinct in the wild

Vulnerable: High risk of becoming endangered in the wild

Near threatened: Likely to become endangered in the near future

Least concern: Lowest risk of becoming endangered

Nature's Heavyweights

Large mammals find it hard to move between the tightly packed trees in the rain forest, so most live in more open areas. However, a few big beasts have adapted to the rain forest habitat.

Endangered Elephants

Herds of forest elephants roam through the African rain forests, but their **habitat** has been destroyed or fragmented, and they are hunted for their **ivory** tusks. Organizations such as WWF (see page 28) are campaigning to stop illegal **poaching** and to protect the elephants' rain forest home.

▼ *Forest elephants are smaller than their grassland cousins. They have darker skin for better* **camouflage***, and their tusks are straighter to stop them from getting caught in the thick undergrowth.*

WHAT DO YOU THINK?

In some parts of the world, rain forests are being cleared to make way for farmland so people can earn money to feed their families. How might these human needs be met without ignoring the needs of rain forest animals?

Little Hippos

Hunting and forest clearance means that only 2,500–3,000 pygmy hippos survive in the steamy **swamps** of West Africa's rain forests. All is not lost for these little hippos, though. The International Union for Conservation of Nature (see page 28) is hoping to make Liberia's hippo habitat a protected area, and they are being bred in zoos all over the world.

▶ *Adult pygmy hippos weigh up to 600 lbs. (275 kg), while common hippos can reach 7,900 lbs. (3,600 kg).*

Rare Rhinos

There are five species of rhinoceros, and all of them are endangered. The two most threatened types are the Sumatran and Javan rhinos, which live in the rain forests of Indonesia. Groups all over the world are fighting to stop them from dying out, including the International Rhino Foundation and WWF. They conduct research, help prevent poaching, and conserve the rain forest habitat.

SAVING WILDLIFE

Javan Rhinoceros

With only 40 to 60 animals left in Java and Vietnam, the Javan rhino is one of the world's most endangered animals. Although everything possible is being done to protect them, experts are afraid that it may be too late to save them from extinction.

Big Cats

Cats can move quietly after their prey through the shadowy darkness of the rain forest. They are also good at climbing, so they can move around in the treetops, too.

Bengal Tiger

In 1900, there were more than 50,000 Bengal tigers, but now there are only 2,500 in the rain forests and grasslands of Asia. They were killed by hunters, and many died as the forests were cut down. The Indian government has set up 66 protected areas, where tiger habitats are conserved. Guards patrol there to deter illegal poaching. These measures may save the tiger from extinction.

Cats in Crisis

Nearly all the big cats of the rain forest are now endangered. Some of them, such as the clouded leopard of Asia, are hunted for their body parts. Tigers, jaguars, and leopards are under threat because their habitat is being destroyed. As they move into smaller areas of rain forest, there may not be enough food to go around.

Cat Conservation

Hunting big cats is now banned in most places. To increase their numbers, some cats may be bred in zoos or wildlife **reserves**. This is called **captive breeding**. It does not always work, though. For example, in zoos, male clouded leopards often kill the females before they can breed.

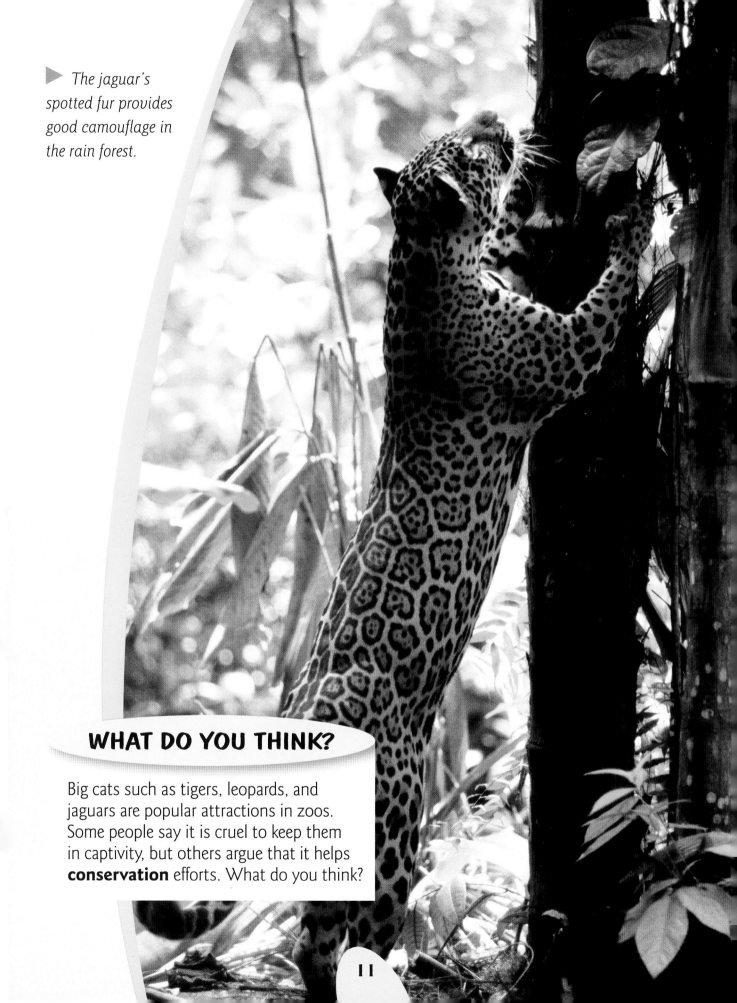

▶ The jaguar's spotted fur provides good camouflage in the rain forest.

WHAT DO YOU THINK?

Big cats such as tigers, leopards, and jaguars are popular attractions in zoos. Some people say it is cruel to keep them in captivity, but others argue that it helps **conservation** efforts. What do you think?

Forest Monkeys and Apes

The rain forest is alive with the calls of many different monkeys and apes, from tiny marmosets to big chimps. It's the perfect home for these treetop travelers.

Great Apes

All species of ape can be found in the rain forests of Africa or Southeast Asia—gorillas, chimpanzees, bonobos, orangutans, and gibbons—and most of them are endangered. Some, such as gibbons, are hunted for their body parts, which are used in Asian medicine. Others struggle to survive in the shrinking areas of available forest.

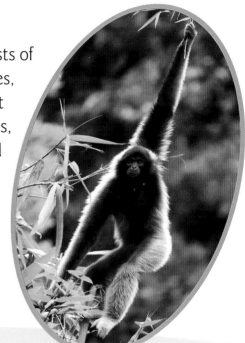

▶ *All species of gibbon are endangered because of hunting and the destruction of their rain forest home.*

Life in the Treetops

Most monkeys live in the canopy, swinging between the trees using their long, strong arms. They can find all the food and shelter they need among the branches, so many of them never come down. Unfortunately, this means that some species have been badly affected by forest clearance. Human **predators** are also a threat. Hunted for its beautiful fur, the golden lion tamarin was nearly extinct by the 1970s, but conservation and captive breeding helped the species survive, and there are now more than 1,000 in the wild.

◀ *Golden lion tamarins are recovering from near-extinction.*

SAVING WILDLIFE

Orangutan

Experts think that there may be only around 10,000 wild orangutans left—half the number there were 10 years ago—because of hunting, **deforestation**, and **wildfires**. These apes can only be found in Sumatra and Borneo, where organizations such as the Orangutan Foundation International are helping save them by planting new trees, preventing illegal mining, and educating locals about the importance of the apes.

Tree Dwellers

The rain forest canopy is so rich with fruit, nuts, leaves, and insects that many animals can get all the food they need in the treetops without ever having to hunt on the forest floor.

Animals of the Canopy

Some of the most curious creatures of the rain forest spend their lives in the tree canopy. The rare binturong of Asia uses its long, muscular tail to grip branches when **foraging** for food. In Madagascar, the unusual aye-aye draws out bugs from trees by tapping on the trunk like a woodpecker. Aye-ayes are killed by local people who think they are bad luck.

▲ *Binturongs have been nicknamed bearcats, although they do not belong to either the bear or the cat families.*

▲ *Algae grows on a sloth's fur to help the sloth blend in with the tree it lives in.*

Sleepy Creatures

Sloths are famous sleepyheads—they hardly move at all. They might come to the ground occasionally, but they are slow-moving and easy prey for big cats and birds of prey such as eagles. To stay out of sight, sloths are **nocturnal**. During the day they stay very still, sleeping upside down on their branches for up to 20 hours a day!

EXTREME ANIMALS

Aye-ayes of the Madagascan rain forest are the only surviving member of the animal family scientists call *Daubentoniidae*.

Lizards Large and Small

Reptiles are cold-blooded, getting the warmth they need to survive from their environment, so tropical rain forests are a favorite place for animals such as lizards and crocodiles.

▲ *Chameleons can change color to blend in with their surroundings or to communicate with other chameleons.*

Little Lizards

All kinds of lizards have **adapted** to life in the rain forest, from giant water monitors to tiny geckos. Iguanas and chameleons have long, sharp claws and long tails that help them grip tree branches. Some can jump from tree to tree in great leaps. Most lizards feed on the plentiful plants and insects, so few are endangered at present.

EXTREME ANIMALS

Flying lizards of Southeast Asia don't actually fly—they use special flaps of skin to help them glide through the rain forest canopy.

Crocs in the Swamps

Crocodiles and caimans lurk in rain forest swamps, feeding on turtles and fish. Their skins are highly prized by hunters, so several species are now endangered, including the black caiman of the Amazon and the small African slender-snouted crocodile.

▼ *Scientists release young Orinoco crocodiles back into the wild in Venezuela.*

SAVING WILDLIFE

Orinoco Crocodile

The largest predator in South America is also one of the rarest. With fewer than 700 Orinoco crocodiles left, they are now a protected species. The Wildlife Conservation Society began a captive-breeding program in the 1990s. Many crocs have been released into the wild, where they are monitored carefully to make sure the males don't kill each other before they can breed.

Tropical Snakes

Snakes are found on every continent except Antarctica—and in a wide range of habitats—but they are most at home in the warm, wet rain forests.

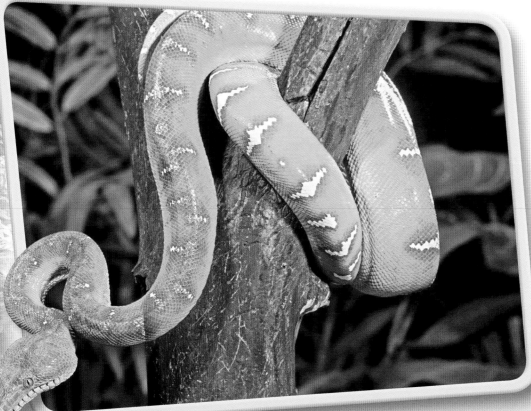

◀ *Emerald tree boas use their coloring to hide in trees so their prey don't spot them.*

Snakes Everywhere

Snakes can be found in most layers of the rain forest. Some coil themselves around branches in the canopy, while others hide in the thick undergrowth or make burrows beneath the soil. There are even some snakes that live in rain forest rivers. Tree snakes like the emerald tree boa, found in the rain forests of South America, tend to be green or brown so they blend in with their leafy habitat. Others, such as the coral snake, have bright colors or patterns on their skin. This is a warning that they are poisonous to stop larger animals from eating them.

Finding Food

Most snakes feed on the plentiful supply of birds, bats, frogs, and insects, but some, such as huge pythons and boa constrictors, can eat much bigger animals. Whatever their favorite snack, when the trees are cut down, all these creatures die or move away, and the snakes' food supply dwindles.

◀ *African bush vipers ambush their prey by hanging from the trees and injecting their victim with venom from their fangs.*

EXTREME ANIMALS

The huge anaconda is the largest snake in the Amazon rain forest, growing up to 30 ft. (9 m) long.

Amphibians

Brilliantly colored frogs, salamanders, and worm-like caecilians are the three main types of amphibians that live in the rain forest. The air is so full of moisture that they don't need pools of water to survive as amphibians do in other habitats.

Threatened Frogs

There are more types of frogs in the rain forest than any other **amphibian**, but they are also the most threatened. The bright colors and poisonous nature of many frogs keep most predators at bay, but more than 100 species have become extinct in the past 30 years because of **climate change** and disease.

Frogs are among the most colorful of all rain forest creatures. This is a red-eyed tree frog in Central America.

EXTREME ANIMALS

The golden poison frog of Colombia contains enough poison to kill several humans.

1 in.
(2.5 cm)

20

Poison Dart Frog

These tiny amphibians are highly toxic—so much so that South American rain forest tribes would tip their hunting spears with the poison. There are many types of poison dart frog, and several of them are threatened by a fungal disease. Conservation programs focus on capturing and treating frogs that have the disease to stop it from spreading.

◄ *Poison dart frogs release a poison through their skin.*

Salamanders in a Warming World

Most salamanders are found in the world's temperate rain forests, but there has been a big drop in their numbers in the past 30 years. Although habitat loss accounts for some of this, experts think they have been more affected by climate change. There is some good news, though: in 2008, three previously unknown salamander species were discovered in the Costa Rican rain forests—and there may be more still undiscovered.

► *Salamanders such as the* Bolitoglossa peruviana *of Ecuador and Peru have webbed feet, so they can cling to smooth surfaces like leaves.*

Minibeasts

Insects are important in the rain forest because they help keep the soil healthy and the flowers pollinated. They also provide food for many larger creatures.

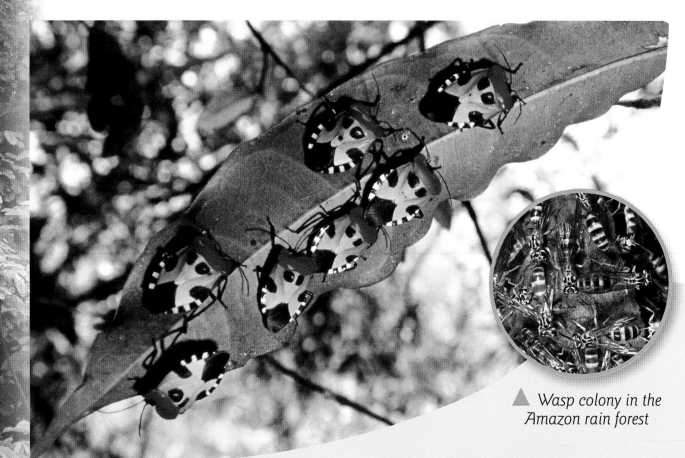

▲ *Wasp colony in the Amazon rain forest*

▲ *These shield bugs in Madagascar release a smelly liquid to stop them from being eaten.*

▼ *Rhino beetle from Malaysia*

Alive with Insects

Huge spiders make their homes on the forest floor and in the trees. Colorful beetles scuttle among the leaves. Ants and termites live in large colonies. Experts think there may be millions of insect species in the rain forest that have not even been discovered! They all contribute to the balance of the rain forest **ecosystem**.

Insects Under Threat

Some insects eat just one type of plant, so if that plant is lost from the forests they have no food. Creepy-crawlies that make their homes in the ground are affected by soil **erosion**. Protecting the rain forests will keep these creatures safe from extinction.

▶ *This colorful weevil sits on a leaf in the rain forest of Papua New Guinea.*

▲ *Banana spider in Hawaii*

SAVING WILDLIFE

Queen Alexandra's Birdwing

The Queen Alexandra's birdwing is the largest butterfly in the world, but it can now only be found in a small area of rain forest in Papua New Guinea. They have been hunted by collectors, and the forest has been cut down for use as farmland. It is now against the law to trade them, and their habitat is protected, so their numbers are rising again.

12 ¼ in. (31 cm)

▶ *Jewel beetles, such as this one from Malaysia, are highly prized by insect collectors.*

In the Air

In the branches of the rain forest trees, thousands of colorful birds feed and breed. High above, birds of prey circle, waiting to swoop on unsuspecting animals below.

Parrot Paradise

Brilliantly colored parrots and toucans are a familiar sight in tropical rain forests. They eat nuts, berries, and insects, and raise their young in tree hollows. While these birds suffer from habitat loss, the biggest danger comes from human hunters, who capture them and sell them as pets.

◀ *Hyacinth macaws, from the Amazon, came under threat because of deforestation and because local tribes killed them to sell their feathers to tourists.*

SAVING WILDLIFE

Hyacinth Macaw
While many macaws are already extinct, the hyacinth macaw is making a comeback from its threatened status. Working with Brazilian authorities, WWF has helped the number of wild hyacinth macaws nearly double in the past 30 years. There are now around 6,500.

▶ *Toucans live in the rain forests of Central and South America.*

Bats in the Night

At night the rain forest air is thick with bats, from giant flying foxes to tiny bumblebee bats smaller than a human thumb. Some bat species are especially important to the rain forest ecosystem because they **pollinate** the flowers.

▲ *Flying foxes and other bats use their clawed feet to hang upside down from branches while sleeping.*

Birds of Prey

Birds of prey such as hawks, eagles, and vultures all live in the rain forest, nesting in the branches of the tallest trees. The harpy eagle of Central and South America is one of the largest— so big that it can catch and carry creatures such as iguanas and sloths.

WHAT DO YOU THINK?

Harpy eagles are a threatened species, but they prey on other endangered rain forest animals such as sloths. Is there a natural order in the wild that we shouldn't interfere with?

Harpy eagle

In the Water

Rain forests are filled with water, from small pools to great rivers. A huge variety of freshwater creatures exist here, from exotic fish to turtles and even dolphins.

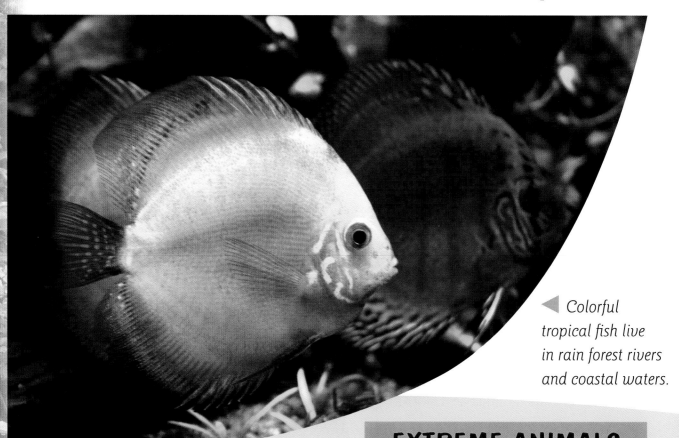

◀ *Colorful tropical fish live in rain forest rivers and coastal waters.*

Tropical Fish

Bright tropical fish flash through the warm forest waters, sharing their habitat with larger species such as electric eels. Recent reports suggest that some species of tropical fish are dying out because they cannot adapt to the rise in water temperatures caused by global warming.

EXTREME ANIMALS

The piranha is the world's deadliest fish. A school of piranhas can strip a victim to the bone in minutes.

8 in. (20 cm)

Pink River Dolphins

Pink river dolphins are one of the creatures affected by the loss of fish in the rain forest waters because they are its main source of food. These Amazonian dolphins are not yet endangered, but they might be in the future if people don't act now to solve the problems of water pollution and dwindling fish stocks.

▶ *Little is known about pink river dolphins, so a lot of research is needed to help in their conservation.*

SAVING WILDLIFE

Manatee

The manatee is the largest marine **mammal** in the Amazon. Manatees are considered vulnerable to extinction because of pollution, hunting, and dam-building. Conservation programs have included rescuing ill or injured manatees and reducing water pollution. But the best hope for the manatee's future is the overall protection of the South American rain forests.

◀ *Manatees look a bit like seals, but their closest living relative is the elephant!*

What Can We Do?

Around 35 rain forest species become extinct every day, but people are more aware than ever before of the threats to rain forest animals, and all over the world there are campaigns to protect this precious environment. Sometimes national governments take steps to protect their endangered creatures. International organizations work with local communities to make a difference. But even individuals can help save rain forest wildlife.

Find out More...

WWF *(www.worldwildlife.org)*
Here you can follow links to information on all kinds of endangered animals and find out what WWF is doing in the world's tropical regions to save these creatures.

Wildlife Conservation Society *(www.wcs.org)*
This U.S. organization manages conservation projects, research, and education programs all over the world. This web site will tell you all about the animals it is working to save, including forest elephants, tigers, and jaguars.

EDGE of Existence *(www.edgeofexistence.org)*
The EDGE of Existence is a special global conservation program that focuses on saving what it calls "Evolutionary Distinct and Globally Endangered" (EDGE) species. These are unusual animals and plants that are under threat.

International Union for Conservation of Nature *(www.iucn.org)*
The IUCN produces the Red List, which lists all the world's known endangered species and classifies them by how threatened they are, from least concern to extinct. You can see the whole list of endangered animals on the web site.

Convention on International Trade in Endangered Species *(www.cites.org)*
CITES is an international agreement between governments that makes sure trade in wild animal species does not threaten their survival. It lists animals that are considered to be under threat from international trading and makes laws accordingly.

International Rhino Foundation *(www.rhinos-irf.org)*
The International Rhino Foundation works in Africa and Asia to protect endangered rhinos and conserve their habitats. On their web site, you can learn all about these creatures and how you can help the IRF.

Do More...

Sign a Petition

Petitions are documents asking governments or organizations to take action on something people are concerned about. Some of the organizations opposite have online petitions that you can sign to show your support for their campaigns.

Go to the Zoo

Find out if your local zoo is involved in any captive-breeding programs and visit them to find out more. Just visiting the zoo helps support these important programs.

Adopt an Animal

For a small contribution to some conservation organizations, you get to "adopt" a rain forest animal. They will send you information about your adopted animal and keep you up to date on all the conservation efforts in the area.

Spread the Word

Find out as much as you can about the threats to rain forest animals and what people are doing to save them, then tell your friends and family. The more support conservation organizations have, the more they can do!

Read More...

Rainforest Food Chains
Food Chains
by Molly Aloian and Bobbie Kalman
(Crabtree Publishing, 2007)

Rain Forests
Our Environment
by Kay Jackson
(KidHaven Press, 2007)

Rain Forests in Danger
Earth SOS
by Sally Morgan
(Sea-to-Sea Publications, 2010)

Tropical Rain Forests
Caring for the Planet
by Neil Champion
(Smart Apple Media, 2007)

Every effort has been made by the publisher to ensure that these web sites contain no inappropriate or offensive material. However, because of the nature of the Internet, it is impossible to guarantee that the content of these sites will not be altered. We strongly advise that Internet access is supervised by a responsible adult.

Rainforest Animals Quiz

See how much you can remember about rain forest animals by taking the quiz below. Look back through the book if you need to. The answers are on page 32.

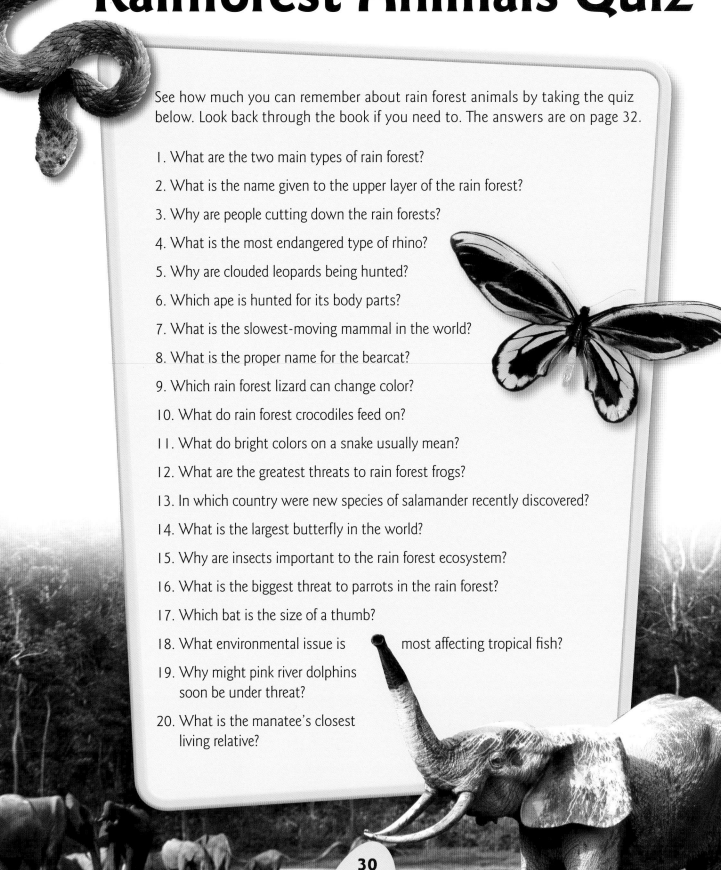

1. What are the two main types of rain forest?

2. What is the name given to the upper layer of the rain forest?

3. Why are people cutting down the rain forests?

4. What is the most endangered type of rhino?

5. Why are clouded leopards being hunted?

6. Which ape is hunted for its body parts?

7. What is the slowest-moving mammal in the world?

8. What is the proper name for the bearcat?

9. Which rain forest lizard can change color?

10. What do rain forest crocodiles feed on?

11. What do bright colors on a snake usually mean?

12. What are the greatest threats to rain forest frogs?

13. In which country were new species of salamander recently discovered?

14. What is the largest butterfly in the world?

15. Why are insects important to the rain forest ecosystem?

16. What is the biggest threat to parrots in the rain forest?

17. Which bat is the size of a thumb?

18. What environmental issue is most affecting tropical fish?

19. Why might pink river dolphins soon be under threat?

20. What is the manatee's closest living relative?

Glossary

adapted changed in order to survive in new conditions

amphibian a cold-blooded animal that spends some of its life on land and some in water

camouflage the color or patterns on an animal that help it blend in with its surroundings

canopy the layer of the rain forest made up of the branches and leaves in the tops of the trees

captive breeding when endangered animals are specially bred in zoos or wildlife reserves so that they can then be released back into the wild

climate the regular pattern of temperature and weather conditions in a particular area

climate change a difference in the expected temperatures and other weather conditions across the world

cold-blooded cold-blooded animals cannot regulate their own body temperature like mammals do, but instead get their warmth from their environment.

conservation efforts to preserve or manage habitats when they are under threat or have been damaged or destroyed

deforestation the cutting down of large areas of forest

domestic tamed by humans; domestic animals are often kept as pets or livestock.

ecosystem all the different types of plants and animals that live in a particular area together with the non-living parts of the environment

endangered at risk of becoming extinct

equator an imaginary line around the middle of the earth that separates the world into the Northern and Southern hemispheres

erosion the wearing away of rock or soil, for example by the motion of water or wind, over a period of time

extinct when an entire species of animal dies out so that there are none left on earth

foraging searching for food or other provisions such as material to build nests or burrows

fragmentation the breaking up of areas of rain forest by cutting down the trees between them

global warming the rise in average temperatures around the world as a result of human activity such as deforestation

habitat the place where a plant or animal lives

ivory the hard, smooth substance that elephant tusks are made from

livestock animals kept by people for meat or milk

logging cutting down trees in the rain forest to sell the wood for building or other uses

mammals warm-blooded animals that give birth to live young

nocturnal active at night

plantations large farms that grow only one type of crop, such as coffee beans or oil palms

poaching hunting an animal when it is against the law to do so

pollinate to transfer pollen from one flower plant to another so that it can make seeds and grow into a new plant

predator an animal that hunts others for food

reptile a cold-blooded animal that lays eggs and usually has scales or plates on its skin

reserves protected areas where animals can roam free and where the environment is carefully maintained for their benefit

species a type of animal or plant

swamps areas of water that are usually filled with plants

wildfires fires that occur naturally but spread very quickly

Index

Numbers in **bold** indicate pictures

Quiz answers

1. Tropical and temperate; 2. Canopy; 3. To use the land for homes, farming, or grazing livestock; 4. Javan rhino; 5. For their body parts; 6. Gibbon; 7. Three-toed sloth; 8. Binturong; 9. Chameleon; 10. Turtles and fish; 11. It is poisonous; 12. Climate change and disease; 13. Costa Rica; 14. Queen Alexandra's birdwing; 5. They keep the soil healthy, pollinate plants, and provide food for other animals; 16. Hunting and capture to be sold as pets; 17. Bumblebee bat; 18. Global warming; 19. Pollution and declining fish stocks; 20. Elephant.